HISTORICAL

THE TEMPLARS

ANDREA PRESS

Publishing Manager
César Álvarez

Editing
Miguel Gómez

English Translation
Rogelio L. Yáñez

English Editing
Charles P. Davis

Published by
ANDREA PRESS
c/ Talleres, 21 - Pol. Ind de Alpedrete
28430 Alpedrete (Madrid)
tel.: 918 57 00 08 - Fax: 918 57 00 48
www.andrea-miniatures.com
andrea@andrea-miniatures.com

Photography
Pag. 6, 7, 14, 15a, 26, 32, 33, 36, 37, 42, 48, 49: Corbis
Pag. 27: Oronoz
Pag. 15b: Album

Illustrations
Francisco Solé
Fuencisla del Amo

Layout
Davidibus

Printed by
Gráficas Europa

D. L.: S. 1212-2004

INDEX

During the first half of the 11th century, Europe experienced a period of tranquillity. The perceived calamities that accompanied the change of millennium, the wars and political upheavals, famine and epidemics had been left behind. An agrarian revolution took place, resulting in improvements in harvesting and thus creating a class of wealthy farmers in rural Europe.

Meanwhile, the Church had to face up to reforms that would help to minimize or, at least, cover up the corruption in the hierarchy.

The church adopted a new policy for the mundane and daily life of the faithful as it sought to consolidate its power. Naturally, this policy confronted the Holy Roman Empire, particularly in German-speaking Europe.

Simultaneously, the Normans were conquering Britain and colonizing Italy and Sicily.

France had fractured into several fiefdoms, with the result that it held no real international power. The Spanish kingdoms were fighting their particular battles with Islam.

Islam was also losing its power and hegemony that had lasted for 300 years across the Middle East, North Africa and Spain. When the Caliphate collapsed, a series of small states or emirates emerged, intent on fighting each other over tribal and regional differences; only Allah held them together.

Byzantium, the third power of the time, succeeded the ancient Roman Empire. With its capital in Constantinople, it held sway over the Balkans, Greece and Anatolia. It practiced a culture more refined than the "barbaric" western Christians; Byzantium has evolved through the centuries in a totally, albeit strange way different from the west.

At the end of the 11tn century Muslims and Christians were dividend in multiple kingdoms, there was only a kingdom state in Europe, Byzantium.

THE WORLD OF MEDIEVAL KNIGHTS

The social structure of medieval Europe revolved around feudalism, where knights fulfilled an important role, one that was much different from the modern romantic notions.

Vassalage was the foundation of this feudal system, an economy based essentially on agriculture and cattle.

It was based, in theory, on loyalty and mutual protection. Vassalage was a symbolic relationship between the Lord and his vassal. The vassal offered to serve the Lord in return for protection, land or favours, according to each case. Moreover, this system worked at all levels of society, from the King down to the humblest peasant.

Society was divided into a number of strata. At the apex of the pyramid sat the King by divine right, next came the nobility and the bishops of the church (feudal lords). Beneath them came the noblemen (hidalgos in Spain), clergy, merchants and artisans (what today would be termed the middle-class) and, finally, the peasants and slaves*.

The king armed his Knights according to a religious rite witch included some religious aspects.

While, even in their day, they were not necessarily slaves, taken in the concept of modern liberty, in essence they were.

The realm was sustained by nobles and, to a great degree, by the church. The Lords could not exist without the peasant's work and, in turn, the peasants needed their Lord's protection to harvest their crops and provide security. The knight belonged to the military nobility and exercised multiple privileges. In theory, these rewards were just compensation for their hard work. Among their duties was the defence of the Church and Catholic faith, to assist the Divine Lord in defending justice throughout the land, protecting widows, orphans and the helpless, and to attend all tournaments and hounds, etc.

All these duties had to be carried out with humble humility, justice, charity and loyalty. Of course, the revenue required for the caring of the horses, maintaining squires, armaments, in addition to his own personal expenses, came from his own purse.

The duties of a medieval knight went beyond those of romantic connotations, at least in theory. They were the defendants of goodwill and social justice.

A knight/lancer consisted of a team of five. The knight was equipped with three to four horses, two mounted squires, and two lightly armed servants who took care of the horses and gave support as archers.

To become a knight, one had to be a member of the nobility and learn how to handle arms and possess the necessary virtues that made up the knightly spirit.

The first step was to become a squire, whose sole mission was to accompany the knight to tournaments and on the battlefield. He became well acquainted with the use of arms, the maintenance of the horses and, of course, the duties of knighthood.

Only if the squire was from a noble family, with adequate finances and was the right age, free from any physical handicap, could he aspire to become a knight after this learning process.

The essence of this medieval society revolved around Christianity, with the knights acting as the Warriors of Christ. As such, they had to attend all religious ceremonies. The ceremony undertaken by a squire ascending to knight was a solemn and profoundly religious act.

The future knight had to remain awake throughout the night in an absorption attitude. He had to be clean and wear his best garments.

On the day of assumption, he took part in the solemn mass, confessing his sins, taking Holy Communion, and listening to a sermon about his obligations within the church. Among these were, of course, the defence of the Faith and goodwill to all men.

On completion of the Mass, he kneeled in front of the altar where he received his sword from the hand of his Godfather. He then received a kiss as a symbol of the honour and responsibilities he would undertake.

The new knight then rode his horse and passed before his close companions. If the circumstances allowed, a tournament then took place along with other celebrations.

For a Templar knight, it can be assumed that the ascension ceremony would have been identical to the one described above. Although, being a monk, he had to detach himself from the mundane, leaving just the highest virtues of the knightly spirit intact.

When doing a pilgrimage to the holy land knights reached the title of crusaders, this allowed them to wear the Red Cross in their shields and clothing.

THE CRUSADERS OF A HOLY WAR

The series of Crusades were military expeditions organized by western Christian kingdoms and sponsored by the Pope in Rome. These took place at intervals from the end of the 11th century to the end of the 13th century, with the sole purpose of rescuing the Holy City of Jerusalem from Islam.

During the First Crusade, the principal objective was achieved by the capture of the Holy City and the creation of a number of Christian states or principalities, among them Edessa, Antioch and Tripoli.

The ensuing Crusades, right up to the eighth, were undertaken to either retain or maintain the success of the first until, eventually, the Franks were expelled from the Middle East.

The Seljuks, an Asian Turkish tribe that had converted to Islam, took control of the Muslim world and continued its expansion until the arrival of Byzantine Anatolia.

The Byzantine Emperor, Alexius, sent a delegation to Rome seeking Pope Urban II's assistance against the Seljuks. The Pope, however, wanted the creation of something more concrete that had nothing to do with the Byzantine interests in the region.

The Clermont Council, held in France, called on the whole of Christendom to take up arms to liberate the Holy Sepulchre, and to re-open the pilgrimage routes closed by the Seljuks. The Church offered indulgences and the pardon of all sins to all who died in pursuit of these aims. In addition, the church offered even more, the right of plunder and dominion over all Muslim conquered land.

The ideal of a crusade, a perfect rendering of the knightly spirit made a deep dent in Medieval Europe, an ignorant society tortured by interminable war, plague and famine. This call to battle was taken up with enthusiasm. To the cry of "God wants", a host of peasants, beggars, pilgrims and the enlightened, totalling close to 20,000, followed their chosen leader, Peter the Hermit, to the Holy

There were eight crusades; only the first one reached the objective of conquering Jerusalem. The following crusades were expeditions to support and delay the inevitable, the lost of the holy sites.

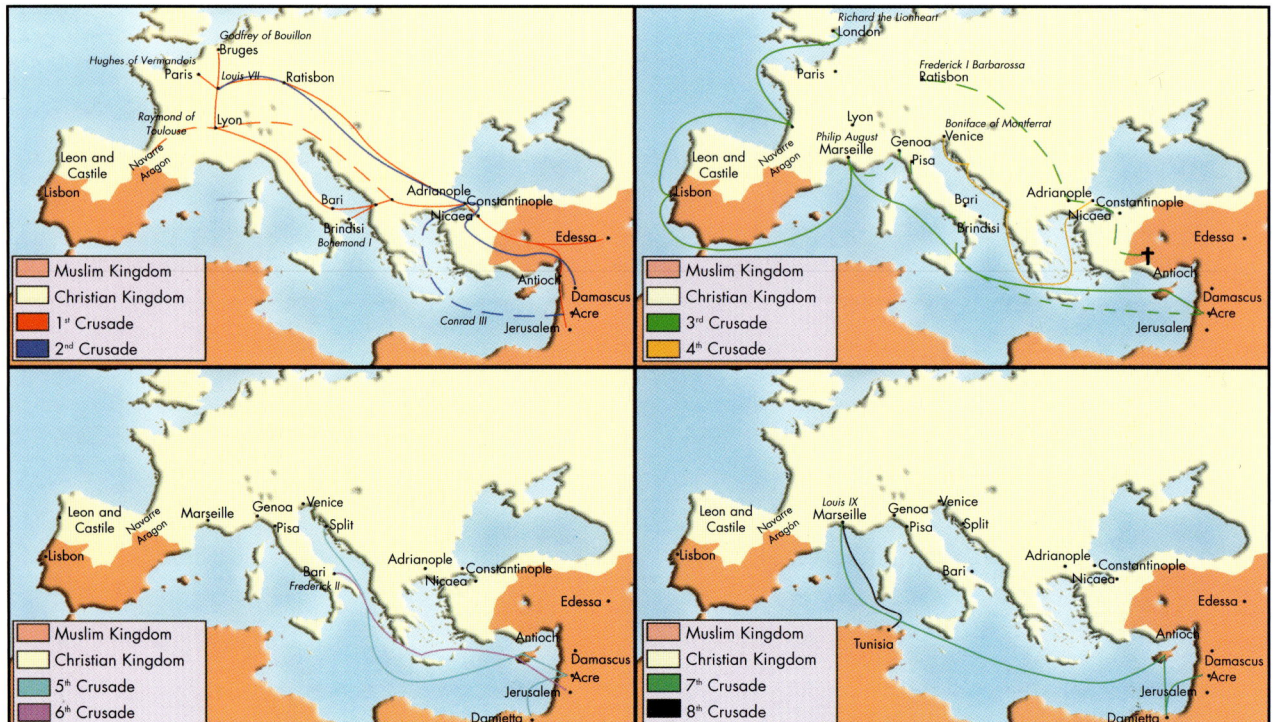

Land. This, so-called, "People's Crusade", undertaken by fanatics, ended in tragedy when they were completely wiped out by the Seljuks.

The military columns led by the Frankish barons followed soon after. They united in Constantinople, where they received a less than warm reception from the Byzantine Emperor. Byzantium always had bad relationships with the West, but the Crusades were beneficial in economic and political terms, thus placing Islamic resistance in the hands of the Crusaders.

Even though they were considered "Brother in Faith", Westerners were generally looked upon as barbarians. They weren't far off the mark, because, during the Fourth Crusade Constantinople was plundered by the Crusaders.

The Emperor wanted to compromise with the Franks with a promise of vassalage over the conquered territories. The Franks, in return, refused any deal and went on to create their own states or independent feuds.

Jerusalem fell to the Crusaders on July 15, 1099. They rapidly took the city, ransacking it, and killing everyone in cold blood.

Godfrey of Bouillon accepted the honour of ruling the city although he refused to accept a crown in the place that Jesus Christ wore a crown of thorns. He adopted the title of "Defender of the Holy Sepulchre" and, by so doing, he prevented Rome's hegemony over the Holy City.

The pious Godfrey died a mere one year later and was succeeded by his brother Baldwin, Count of Edessa. He wished to be crowned King of Jerusalem with the support of the Church and the Frankish barons.

It was at this point in history that the Kingdom of Jerusalem and the Frankish Principalities entered into a permanent battle with Islam.

The life of the Crusader was a precarious one, constantly threatened by war and relying for his security on a handful of romantic-minded knights.

However, this pure, aesthetic ideal was always questionable. The values of knighthood had been diluted by dissolute living, intrigue and jealousy among the Frankish barons. It was not long before the possibility of retaining the island of Christianity in a Muslim sea was lost.

CHRONOLOGY

THE FIRST CRUSADE. 1095 – 1099 AD
The First Crusade, led by "Peter the Hermit", was called "The People's Crusade".
This disorganised rabble was wiped out by the Turks. The Frankish nobles went on to conquer Jerusalem.

THIRD CRUSADE. 1189 - 1192
Following the capture of Jerusalem by Saladin, a Third Crusade was organized. Among the kings who took part was the English king, Richard the Lion Heart.

THE FIFTH CRUSADE. 1217 – 1221 AD
This Crusade was led by John of Brienne, the exiled King of Jerusalem. His only major victory was the capture of the Egyptian port of Damietta.

THE SEVENTH CRUSADE. 1248-1254 AD
Called "Saint Louis's Crusade", after Louis IX of France. He was defeated in Egypt and held prisoner by the Sultan. He eventually gained his freedom after paying a ransom.

THE SECOND CRUSADE. 1147 – 1149 AD
The Second Crusade was preached by Saint Bernard of Clairvaux. It was led by the German Emperor, Conrad III, and King Louis VII of France.

THE SIXTH CRUSADE. 1022 – 1029 AD
This peaceful Crusade was led by the German Emperor, Frederick II, who negotiated with the Sultan of Egypt to re-open the Christian pilgrimage routes to Jerusalem.

THE FOURTH CRUSADE. 1202 – 1204 AD
Pope Innocent III, together the Doge of Venice, organized this crusade. The crusaders plundered the city of Constantinople, capital of Byzantium.

THE EIGHTH CRUSADE. 1270 AD
Once again organized by Louis IX of France. The Crusade was cut short by his death from cholera while preparing to attack Tunis.

THE ORDER'S FOUNDATION

One of the biggest problems for the Franks in the Middle East was the problem of affording protection to the pilgrims. After all, this was one of the underlying reasons behind the Pope's purpose of raising the ideal of the Crusades in the first place. That, and to give security and access to all Christian pilgrims to the holy sites.

Once the coastline had been secured, accessing Jerusalem by sea was assured. But, communication between the Frankish kingdoms or visiting the holy sites necessitated a dangerous and risky journey constantly harassed by bandits and Saracens.

The lack of troops and military resources of the new Christian kingdoms were hardly adequate to offer protection anywhere beyond city walls or fortresses. The Templar order was established with the sole purpose of affording armed protection to all Christian pilgrims.

In 1118, under the rule of King Baldwin II, a small group of knights decided to take vows of chastity, poverty and obedience to the Patriarch of Jerusalem.

The two leaders of these nine knights were Hugh of Payns and Godfrey of Saint-Omer. In the beginning, they decided to call their new order "The Poor Fellow-Soldiers of Jesus Christ".

The King gave them barracks on the south side of

the Temple of Solomon. This move prompted them to change their name, first to "The Knights of the Temple of Solomon", followed by "The Knights of the Temple", then just to "The Templars" or simply "The Temple".

On acceptance of this royal favour, the King gave them the honourable and important mission of maintaining all roads and paths free between the cities and holy sites of the Holy Land.

The first decade of the order's existence were marked by lack of any activity due to the vows of poverty vows they had taken. The Members of the Order had to beg for food and clothing and the charity of the faithful.

They had no resources that would seduce new volunteers and they were unable even to wear the typical white cloak adorned with the Red Cross that would later be their trademark.

Indeed, It was an impossible task to accomplish with so few men. A mere nine knights were hardly enough to maintain the roads clear of bandits and Saracens. However, in time the Order began to prosper.

King Baldwin II was enthusiastic about the order in which he saw the pure ideas of knighthood. The Order was awarded tax exemptions and they were assigned to protect the Count of Champagne who came from Hugh of Payne's hometown.

Once the Order started to get on solid ground, it was evident it needed to establish its headquarters in the West, away from the precarious situation in Jerusalem constantly threatened by enemies.

It needed to create an economic thread of support and promotion among the noble families of Europe who ruled, along with the Church, the politics of the world at that time.

Jerusalem, 30 A.D. Salomon's temple was on the back of the city, it quartered the first Templars.

FIRST TEMPLARS

Its founder, Hugh of Payns, arrived from Europe in 1128 and immediately started the journey to seek support for his new Order.

Hugh of Payns, seen on foot in the illustration, came from the city of Troyes in the French Champagne. He was born around 1080 to a noble house related to the Count of Champagne and the future Saint Bernard of Clairvaux. He received, from an early age, a Christian and military education and learned the role of the knights that he would inherit. Even as a teenager he was attracted to the aesthetic life of the monks and to religious ceremonies.

Hugh joined the First Crusade when he was 20 years old. He soon found that there were no problems discovering people with similar interest among the fellow Crusaders.

It isn't difficult to imagine those young knights, entering into a Holy War and approaching the sublime as a warrior monk; ardent, brave and idealistic, prepared to forfeit their lives to liberate the Holy Sepulchre.

Hugh of Payns instinctively knew how to teach his eight companions the ideal of resigning the mundane and to seek a more transcendent and superior mission.

A religious mission based on the bearing of arms, in itself a contradiction in terms, A contradiction, however, that was resolved by Saint Bernard of Clairvaux. He was a powerful Cistercian abbot who assisted the young knight to obtain the apostolic confirmation and who set out the rules for the new Order.

Hugh of Payns was well up to the task of handling all the political threads when drafting new members and seeking help in Europe and from the Church.

At the Council of Troyes, the Order obtained the Pope's support and approval of the Templar's rules. In the years following the Council of Troyes, Hugh and his companions continued to promote the Order.

Next to the opulence and indolence of the noble, the new Order offered a life of purity. These warrior monks also attracted a small number of nobles that couldn't inherit land and also felt no attraction for material possessions. The Templar ideal gave sense to their lives in tune with the forgotten ideals of the medieval knight.

The enthusiasm for the new Order even reached the powerful Lords of the time who gave big donations. These later became known as "Templar parcels". Furthermore, they also donated monasteries, farms and quarters thus assuring the base for the economic future of the Order.

Pope Innocent II was a great admirer and protector of the order. In 1139, he published his Omne Datum Optimun bull consolidating the Order and giving them independence of any temporal or ecclesiastic power and putting them under the exclusive mandate of the Holy See. Henceforth, they answered for their acts only to the Pontiff himself.

Two knights on a horse

This illustration is based on one of the Templar's seals.

As mentioned earlier, the first Templars, having taken the vows of poverty, did not wear the white cloak or the Red Cross in the beginning. It was not until 1147 that Eugene III awarded the Order this "uniform". They were to wear it as a "triumphant shield that kept them strong against the infidel".

The main idea behind this image of piety and poverty was to remember those vows behind the founding of the Order. Unfortunately, these vows did not last long.

Another version of the same illustration, tells us that the two knights represent the double vocation of the Order; the military and the religious.

This temporal and spiritual duality is shown as the white and black colours in their banner or "Beauseant", black for earth and white for sky i.e. mundane knights and God's knights.

These knight brothers ride horses carrying the black and white banner that they call Beauseant' because "they are full of love for the friend of Christ and black and terrible for their enemies".

RULES OF THE TEMPLARS

The Templars rules were based on the concepts adopted at the Council of Troyes by Hugh of Payns.

They were clearly based on religious ideals, by the ideology of Saint Bernard of Clairvaux and the Cistercian monks.

It is a meticulous text ruling every religious and military aspect of the brotherhood. It is also complemented by a number of hierarchical statutes that are discussed later. Over the proceeding 150 years, the text continually evolved, finally reaching over 600 articles.

The Templar rules did not allow any members freedom of initiative.

This gave cohesiveness to the troops, and was something completely innovative to any Christian army of the time, where each knight did everything according to his own criteria.

The monastic vow of obedience gave the Order a religious character. Any misconduct or insubordination was seen as a sin in the Templar's mind.

Among their multiple articles and dispositions, can be emphasized the following:

- Novices were first accepted for a probationary period. If the Grand Master and the Brothers were pleased, he was allowed to express his aspiration "with a pure heart" before the Council of the Brotherhood.
- There were two types of council. The General Council, where all important matters were decided, including the election of the Grand Masters, and the Ordinary Council, held weekly if there were more than four brothers.
- All knights should eat in the refectory in silence whilst listening to the Holy Texts.
- No children were allowed in the Order.
- The dress code was strict in every aspect. It had to be austere and functional, excluding any kind of jewelry, gold or silver ornaments.
- The Grand Master controlled all of the Brother's goods, and he exercised maximum authority over the Order.
- If one of the members was sick, he could be

The order's seal, showing two knights on a single horse.

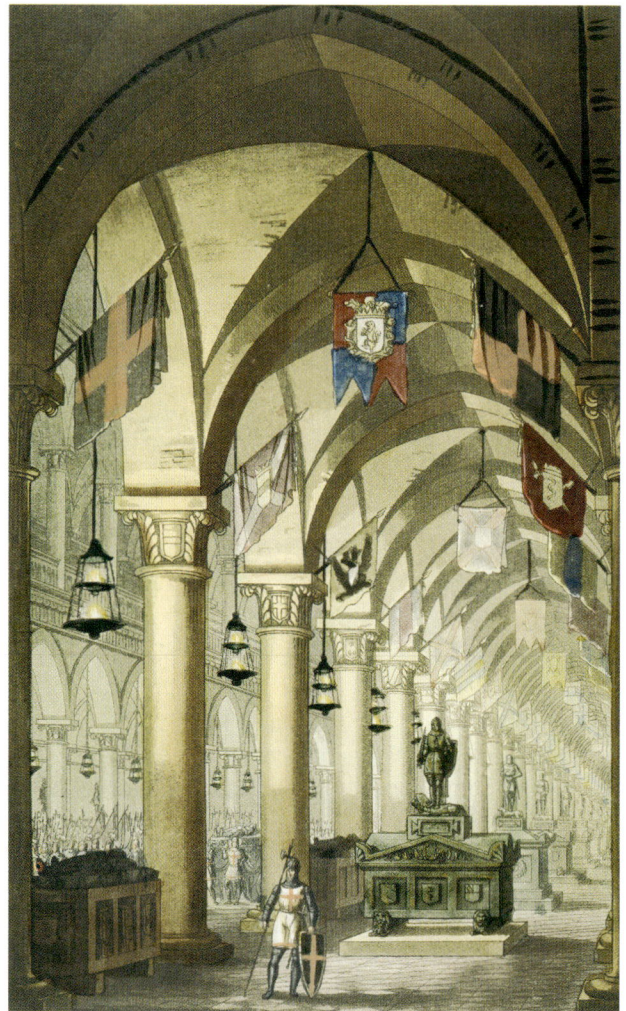

There were two chapters:
General, for important matters and Ordinary for the daily life.

The Church blessed the swords and the killing of Muslims.

relieved of attending religious ceremonies, though still attending daily prays. They were attended to in separate hospitals.

- Hunting and archery were forbidden. The only animal allowed to be hunted was the lion (!).
- Without the Grand Master's consent, no one was allowed to have a bag (purse) or a locked chest; nor were they allowed mail from relatives or any other person.
- When a Brother committed a small misdemeanour, as when talking in combat or in any other circumstance, he had to personally present himself before the Grand Master and beg for penance.

If the misdemeanor was too big, he was banished from the company while waiting for the Grand Master's decision.

- If the fault was serious, and the Brother in question expressed no regret, he was banished from the rest of the group "the pious cattle" i.e. "We must banish the immoral from the group".

- "Indulgence should not be bigger than the fault itself nor the punishment smaller that make the sinner to repeat the fault."
- The Order was considered as something born from the Holy Scriptures and the Divine Providence in the Holy Land. For that reason, they could kill any enemy of the Cross without committing a sin. They could keep land and slaves, villains and fields and rule them in justice.
- All of the Order's resources were organized into provinces with a Knight Commander in charge.
- Over time, the Templars ruled over ten provinces. There were three in the Middle East, Jerusalem, Antioch and Tripoli. There were also seven provinces in Europe, France, Britain, Poitou, Aragon, Portugal, Hungary and Apulia.
- There was a chance to join the Order for a short period of time, although all rules should be followed.
- Women were not allowed in the Order and consorting in any way with women was forbidden.
- They were not allowed to enter cities, towns or castles in a 5 km. radius from their headquarters. Older knights were not allowed to retain their military equipment; they had to give it away to other brothers. IN return, a docile horse was given to them so they could spend their time taking care of the animal.

Templar architecture was functional and austere, much like the order's spirit.

THE WARRIOR MONK

This illustration shows Saint Bernardo of Clairvaux, in company with a number of Templar monks, during one of the many missions in France.

Saint Bernard's influence in medieval Christendom and over the Templars, was enormous. He was a friend and relative of Hugh of Payns. It was he who assisted Hugh in writing the Templar's rules and who wrote the homily "PRAISE TO THE NEW MILITIA", where he compares the Templars' values with those of the "castle" knights who were "more interested in young ladies than attending their military duties".

Young Bernard de Fontaines from Burgundy joined the Cistercian Order in 1112. He was ordered to found and take care of the Clairvaux Abbey in Champagne. From the most humble works to the spiritual guidance of all Templars, everything he did, he did with piety and devotion.

Besides being very young, his profound intelligence and oratorical qualities made him an irresistible influence.

He wrote letters to Kings, Popes and Bishops. He further wrote several treaties on theology, aestheticism and on Christian knighthood. He preached throughout Europe, in the highest courts and monasteries. He talked about Christ and the Virgin Mary in a candid and military way. He expressed, in the most erudite manner, what medieval society embarked on the Crusades wished to hear.

In his homily "PRAISE TO THE NEW MILITIA", he wrote "Christ's soldiers fight the Lord's battles with confidence, without fear of committing sin when killing an enemy and without any mistrust of obtaining eternal salvation if killed.

To kill, or to be killed for Christ did not imply a sin in eyes of God.

It is a glorious moment; in the first case, men fight for the Lord and, in the second case, the Lord (Christ) give himself up to the men as a gift looking with good eyes what he has done with the enemy and, above all, Christ offers himself as solace to those who die in combat.

So, we can say it once and a thousand times, all Christ's knights kill with confidence and die with even more confidence.

He gains plenty if he dies and a triumph for Christ if he wins."

Daily life in the monastery

At midnight all the bells rang the call for "matins" (meet). All brothers had to rise, put on their shoes and wear a cloak to attend the religious ceremony that consisted of reciting 13 "Holy Fathers".

After completing the recital, they then had to prepare to the stables and do what was necessary. After that, they recited another "Holy Father", and then returned to bed.

At the "Prima" (First Ring), they dressed and attended Mass. When Mass was over, they then attended to their duties. It must be borne in mind, these monasteries were not only places of worship and military training, they were also farms and barracks.

They were centres for both agricultural and cattle, with large tracts of land and they employed many peasants. The knights took great care of their arms and other military accoutrements. They also had to keep their bodies fit by strict military training.

The first meal of the day was at lunchtime. The Knights and Sergeants were the first to eat. After them came the squires, servants and "turcopoles" (mercenary soldiers from Syria).

There was a rule that laid down that two knights should eat from a single plate, although each carried his small bowl, a spoon and bread knife. Eating was done in silence and no one could leave their seat until the end of the meal, with the sole exception of a call to arms, a bloody nose or if horses were fainting in the stable.

In the afternoon, they would pray the "Norms" and "the afternoon prayers" and, of course, continue with the normal work.

Following "afternoon prayers", it was time for dinner.

As the final bells of the day rang the "completas", the whole community repaired to the chapel where the Field Marshal and the Knight Commander give out their instructions for the following day.

After checking the stables, the animals, and giving the squires their instructions for the morrow, the Brothers retired to bed.

TEMPLARS RANKS

The Order's established hierarchy allowed them a systematic and well-organized army in the Holy Land.

Besides the necessary number of knights required to defend the fortresses and reinforcements in the principal headquarters, there were up to 300 well-trained knights ready for combat at a moments notice.

In addition to these 300 men, there were also sergeants, squires and turcopoles (mercenary Syrian horsemen of the Temple), which, together totaled close to 3000 men. Not even the King of Jerusalem could command such an army ready for any event.

GRAND MASTER (XIII century)
He acted as sovereign and exercised great powers, although he was under the Chapter's authority when dealing with important issues; he possessed just one vote on the council.

SENESCHAL (XIII century)
He was the Order's second dignitary and in charge of the Quartermaster Corps. He had privileges similar to the Grand Master.

FIELD MARSHAL (XIII century)
He was responsible for the knight's training and was the highest authority during wartime.

KNIGHT COMMANDER (XIII century)
They were in charge of the provinces. The Jerusalem Knight Commander was the Order's treasurer.

TAILOR (XIII century)
His mission was to provide all knights with clothing, in keeping with the time of the year.

KNIGHT BROTHERS (XIII century)
Each had the right to 3 horses, a squire and his own tent.

KNIGHT SERGEANT BROTHERS (XIII century)
These were members of plebeian origins. Each had the right to one horse.

SUB-FIELD MARSHAL (XIII century)
He was under the Knight Marshal's command and all sergeants were under his direct command. He was a sergeant, but received similar treatment to a knight.

BANNER HOLDER (XII century)
He was a sergeant and an official who commanded all squires, sentinels and explorers.

TURCOPOLIER (XIII century)
He was an official in change of the mercenary Syrian cavalry, or turcopoles.

SQUIRE (XIII century)
His mission was to assist the knight during combat, taking care of the knight's equipment and horses.

BROTHER KNIGHTS, BROTHER SERGEANTS

In this next illustration, can be seen a mounted Sub-Marshal or Chief of Sergeants, a Templar knight and a turcopole mercenary.

Although there were many squires, servants, vassals and auxiliary troops; knights of noble origin and brother sergeants (of plebeian origin) were the core of the Order. To enter the Temple, a meticulous initiation rite had to be passed.

The would-be Knight or Templar Sergeant had to pass several tests before being allowed to enter the Order.

It was a purification and cleaning process, where the would-be member broke from the sensual world and was reborn into the more dignified life of truth and service. The acolyte's strength and tenacity was put to the test by long meditation, fasting and maintaining vigil over the Cross.

The Knight Commander reunited the Chapter in the unit's chapel and asked if anyone opposed the new novice.

If this request was answered with silence, the novice was called and placed in a chamber close by.

Two or three Brothers interviewed him and related how hard life was for a Templar, and explained the entire test that he had to pass before full acceptance.

After the interview, he took an extensive, detailed questionnaire that he had to answer in a sincere and humble way.

It was a test to explore his mind and determine his sincerity about joining the Order.

Once he had finished the questionnaire, he was requested to leave the chamber. Then, if nobody opposed his entrance, he joined the brothers once again. He was then asked some more practical questions: Are you married or engaged? Do you belong to any other Order? Do you have any debts you are unable to pay? Are you in good physical shape? Are you of noble birth? (If he was to be a knight) or, Are you a free man or the slave of another man (this was asked of the aspiring sergeants), and many more questions?

Once these obstacles were overcome, the Knight Commander placed on him the cloak of the Order. Then some psalms were recited and each brother recited a Holy Father.

When this was over, the Knight Commander raised the candidate, who was on his knees, and gave him a peace kiss on the lips, as was the custom of the day. At this point, the ceremony was complete.

The Knight Commander courteously says to the new brother, "Beautiful Brother, our Lord Jesus Christ has taken your desires and has placed you in this great company of Templar knights. Put all your efforts in maintaining it."

Basic equipment

As it will be seen in the following pages, Templar military equipment underwent many changes throughout its two centuries of existence.

Basically, the weapons of a Knight Brother consisted of the following: A chain mail coat, some mesh shoes, a helmet and an iron skullcap that was placed on the chain mail covering the head and neck, leaving the face open. He had a double-edged sword with a rounded tip, a lance, a shield, a Turkish mallet and a knife or dagger.

Under the chain mail he wore a corselet. Over this, he wore a white mantle, if he were a Knight, or a black mantle, if he was a Sergeant. He had two shirts, two long underpants, two pair of shoes, soap, a fur-lined jacket and two cloaks, one for winter and another for summer, a short tunic and a clock.

For the bed, there was a mattress, three sheets and a wool blanket, and a bedspread. In addition, they received three valises, two to hold supplies, and one of leather for the chain mail.

There were also two towels and kitchen equipment: a kettle, a measurer, two knives, two glasses, two bottles, a scraper and an axe.

The sergeants received identical equipment, although they did not have the small personal stove issued to the knights.

Jolé-Amo

EVOLUTION OF TEMPLAR ARMAMENT AND EQUIPMENT

XI CENTURY

1. Double-edged fighting sword or "great sword".
2. Battle axe. Mace
3. Crossbow
4. Turkish bow.
5. Sling
6. Wooden, leather-covered shield.
7. Norman chain-mail.
8. Chain-mail.

1. - The arms, shields and tactics of Crusaders and the Templars evolved greatly during the two centuries of Frankish occupation. Christians and Muslims influenced and learnt from each other.

Most of the northern European knights wore chain mail as body armour. Chain mail was constructed of thousands of metal rings, each hooked together to another four rings.

Originally, chain mail coats were very long, as they reached to below the wearer's knees. With the passing of time, they became shorter, eventually reaching halfway above the knees, and were worn over a leather or cloth shirt. Later, this shirt became cushioned cotton cloth to better protect the body from the metal.

The majority of the sergeants and poorer warriors had no sleeves to the chain mail. Most, in fact, wore a short-sleeved shirt that left their forearms unprotected. With time, the arms too became totally covered. Even the legs eventually became covered with metal wedges that were tied around the back of the leg with laces.

The chain mail surcoat was complimented with a cap that was secured to the head by means leather straps. During subsequent evolutions, the head, too, became totally covered leaving only openings for the eyes.

XII CENTURY

1. A knight's full suit of armour Belt and shoulder belt or baldrick.
2. Baldrick.
3. Evolved crossbow.
4. Infantry shield.
5. Round shield
6. Cavalry lance.
7. Muslim swords.
8. Infantry pike.
9. Complete helm.
10. Norman helmet with face guard.
11. Infantry helmet.

Most of the knights wore a cushioned leather or cloth cap on their heads to protect the skull from the metal of the chain mail cap.

The vast majority of the knights carried a simple metal helmet, with a band around the rim. Sometimes, the helmet was constructed from a number of metal sheets. Helmets, too, evolved to the point where they covered the whole head, leaving just a small opening for the eyes.

2. - Between the XI and XII centuries, a kite-shaped shield was used by mounted troops. It was designed to protect the left flank from shoulder to feet. The infantry were equipped with lighter shields, rounded or flat at the base to allow them to be set on the ground.

The shield also evolved over time, becoming smaller and lighter, specially the ones used by the cavalry, to allow the horseman to see over. In the beginning, the shield was decorated with the knight's ornaments, but during the XII century, heraldic colours were added.

The Templar rules proscribed any form of decoration on the armour, spurs, or on arms in general, putting a stop to traditional, ostentatious military displays.

XIII CENTURY

1. Shield
2. Turkish mace.
3. Closed helm
4. Shoulder protection
5. Sword and scabbard.
   An Ottoman belt.
6. Flail
7. Armour covering
   the upper shoulder.
8. Grieves, to protect
   the leg from knee
   to ankle.
9. Battle axe.
10. Sword with scabbard
    and baldrick.
11. Lance with banner.
12. Pike
13-14. Bascinets.

3. - The sword was considered the most noble of all arms. Of course, its efficiency depended, in great part, on the ability of the user.

It had to be well balanced, with its mass distributed throughout the length. It weighed from 1.3 to 3 kgs. It was hand-forged in hard, flexible steel with a core of ductile iron.

During the clamour of battle, when fighting was too close and difficult to swing the sword, other weapons were used. Among these was the battleaxe that came in different configurations: with different types of blade and hooks or with a hammer in the back. These fell from favour when firearms came into use.

The Turkish mace was one of the most feared weapons;

rotating it to gain leverage, its impact could crush bones and skulls, and smash through armour.

The crossbow possessed both power and precision, and was much better than a conventional longbow. It was so deadly, that the church forbade its use in the XI century. It greatest advantage was that the crossbowman, unlike the longbow man, required no long training and it did not need strength to load.

There were two types of lances: a small one, derived from the infantry pike, and a larger one, equipped with a counter-weight, used by the knights.

4. –During the XI century, the supremacy of the mounted knight, without doubt, reached its peak. Combat by lance

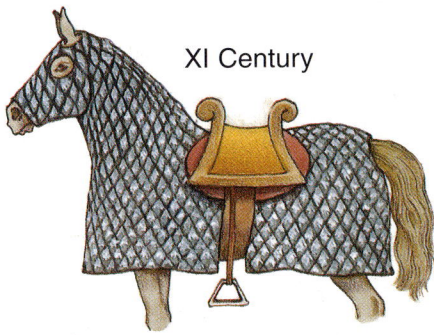

XI Century

XI Century

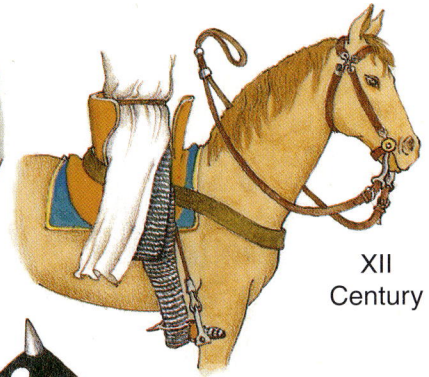

XII Century

XII Century

XII Century

XII Century

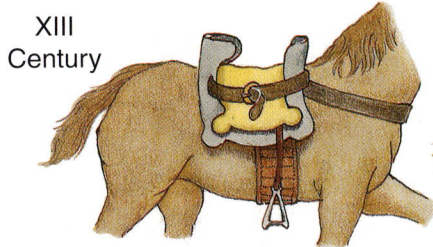

XIII Century

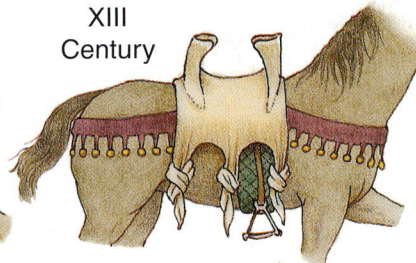

XIII Century

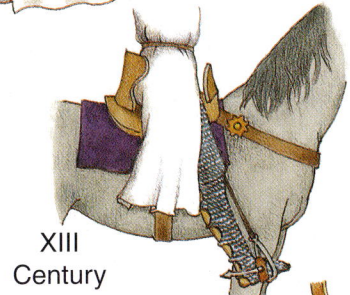

XIII Century

Bridle, XIII Century

Halter

XI Century

XII Century

XIII Century

was developed by the Norman cavalry and, when introduced, was revolutionary on European battlefields.

Besides all the advantages of heavy cavalry, the light cavalry became more and more popular. It was mainly used by the Muslim armies and by the Christian armies in Iberia.

Light cavalry, horsemen who rode with short stirrups and legs held close to the horse, made horse handling and movements much easier.

Meanwhile, Norman cavalry extended the use of the long stirrup and the tight-fitting saddle, with a cushioned lining, that ensured that the knight was held tight.

This type of mount, with the legs stretched was dubbed the "bridle mount", and allowed the horsemen to remain in the saddle even when charging and the ensuing violent clash. Double girths were used to make sure that the saddle remained tight to the horse.

During the XII century, knights once again began covering their horses with cloth or leather to protect them from arrows or wounds inflicted by the infantry.

All this protection, the caparison, eventually became cushioned and increased the horse's protection. Sometimes, even chain mail caparisons were used, similar to the ones used in ancient times by Greeks, Romans and Persians.

The halters for the mules and pack animals were not equipped with a bit. This was because the animal was not required to be directed with the precision of a horse in battle.

TEMPLAR CASTLES

Templar church of La Vera Cruz; close to Segovia's Alcazar. (Spain).

Irak des Chevaliers forteresses' armes court yard.

Mousayliha castle on the Nahr el Jaouze valley (Jordan).

The whole of the Crusader territories were Christian bastions in the middle of Islam and, since the beginning, were exposed to attacking forces.

These bastions were situated in northern Syria and in south and central Turkey They had been abandoned by the Byzantines long before. There were many fortified ports and fortresses along the coastline of Syria and Palestine.

In these areas, there was not much to do the existing fortresses except renovate them.

However, in central Syria, Libya and Palestine there were no fortification, so here the Franks built their own castles.

Fortifications were constructed according to the immediate needs. For example, there were "siege fortresses" built to withstand a long siege.

Basically, the knights needed to fortify their camp. To do this, they built a series of small castles, allowing them to control all access and communications. There were also small, practical castles that served as a refuge and for provisioning the knights, especially during campaigns when they were far from their headquarters. Both types of castle served as outposts once a particular campaign was over.

In addition, there were large, extremely solid castles that, over time, turned into political centres. From these, the Lord or Baron ruled his territory, making it easy to manage, to colonize and make economic progress.

The castles situated along the border were the most useful and necessary for the survival of the Frankish states. Of course, it was these fortresses that were the most exposed to attack and, it was these castles that were maintained under strict military rule.

The Crusades became a cultural phenomenon influencing both Eastern and Western cultures. The development of the architecture of war eventually made it difficult to distinguish between Christian and Muslim elements.

The Crusaders introduced the "Homage Tower" as

part of their eastern castles that was something completely new. Along with, because of the scarcity of wood, all the castles were built completely out stone.

The Crusader fortresses were built, pretty much, along the same lines as the Muslim ones.

The lack of wood made the builders use stone vaults that weren't too high, only two stories with thick walls and very few openings.

The main Templar castles in the Holy Land were:

"Chastel-Pelerin" (Pilgrims' Castle), built in 1218 by the Knight Master William de Chartres.

"Chastel-Blanc" (White Castle) in Safet, built in 1240. This was a large fortress quartering up to 1,700 knights and their auxiliary troops during peacetime, and 2,200 during wartime.

Tortoise, a triple-structure castle built on the shoreline.

Saint John of Acre, a fortified palace flanked by four towers topped by four brilliant lions.

Beaufort, acquired in 1260, had an excellent view over the Vahar valley towards the sea and the port of Tyre.

The northern outposts of Port Bonnel and Gastein (Baghras), and many others of lesser importance, spread throughout the Holy Land to quarter men and munitions. The Templar fortresses are distinguished from the Hospitaller ones by, among other things, their square or rectangular towers.

These square towers were vulnerable to mines and projectiles as they had a large "dead zone" on the front façade that couldn't be covered by archers.

To solve this problem, the Templars united the tower to the longest wall of the fortress, like Tortosa Castle. The other way to avoid dead angles was to introduce a round tower, although they were much more difficult to build and required advanced technical knowledge. They also created difficult living conditions and were hard to mount war equipment.

Ponferrada (Leon), Spain. Templar castle. Important headquarters on the Iberian Peninsula, with very few military functions, the border with Islam moved very rapidly to the south.

CHAPEL

STABLES

FOOT SOLDIERS'
LIVING QUARTERS

GUARDHOUSE

DRY MOAT

THE SEP

CATTLE STALLS

GREAT HALL

KITCHEN

STORE HOUSES

Solé-Amo

SIEGE MACHINERY

As the title suggests, most people associate medieval siege engineering with siege machines. These ingenious machines could also be used for defending the fortresses. In fact, it was common to bombard the enemy from the towers.

One of the first stone throwers was called "mandrones". These were simple catapults crewed by around 20 men throwing ropes simultaneously from the opposite side of the counterweight. The simple design and small size made it an essential part of the Muslim armies and it was used extensively.

During the XIII century, the Crusaders attained the acme of perfection when building catapults, with Templars building the best ones. For example, during the Damietta siege, the Templar catapult "The Mufrite" caused desolation and fear among the city's defendants. By means of adjustable shot, it could propel rocks to short targets as well as to those further away. This meant that the besieged could do little to defend themselves against it.

Time chroniclers are amazed at the perfection of the Templar machines. The brothers were meticulous in everything they did, and their military machines were no exception. For their design, they got the best engineers of the time, mainly from Armenia, architects and specialized craftsmen.

Another siege machine was the mobile wooden tower, that along with the battering ram was most used by the Crusaders. However, the tower has a serious drawback, it was very easy to set alight by using Greek fire; it was also very difficult to transport because of its great size.

The Muslims were not enamoured with the tower. When the Crusaders left the Holy Land, the towers stopped being used in any war.

Different techniques were used by both sides when undertaking a siege. They included mines, trenches and digging under the walls.

TEMPLARS IN WAR

The Templar war scenario did not just take place in the Middle East. Christianity also had another Crusade against Islam, on the Iberian Peninsula, and the warrior monks could fight there without resigning their vows.

Their bravery and effectiveness in combat was evident from the start. So much so that monarchs entrusted their castles and fortresses to them on the borders of Islam.

Donations by royal and noble houses got bigger in terms of land, castles, rents and one fifth of all conquered land. The Christian territory in Spain became dotted with castles and Templar tracts.

The Templars success story spawned a school of followers in Spain, including the Calatrava and Santiago Orders. When the Templars were accused of heresy and were dissolved, many a Brother received assistance from these orders.

Templars received a warm welcome in Spain and Portugal. The conditions of war in Spain made it an

Armies were followed by the necessary provisioning.

Templar's bravery pushed them in several occasions to make suicidal cavalry charges against Muslim armies much greater in numbers.

idyllic scenario for these monks to develop their Order.

Templars monks participated in the Mallorca conquest and, in consequence, received 20 percent of the territory and a castle near Palma.

Donation flooded in to the Templars from various Royal houses and this cannot just be attributed to their devotion or admiration for the Soldiers of Christ. Templars were an invaluable force for conquering territories and were very close to being a standing army. Kings were very interested in having them on their territories and the Templars, in return, gained in power each time they fought and won a battle or subdued a castle.

The Templar Order took part in most of the battles in Syria, Palestine, Egypt. Each time, the sole objective was to defend the conquered territory.

At the same time, they often entered into alliances with their Muslim opponents; a situation that was

Even though they have a tremendous Muslim pressure, Franc knights got time to fight among each other.

looked down upon by their co-religionists who, at times, called these deals treasonous.

These policies of alliances with Muslims powers was not well thought of in the Christian World, especially the one with the sect of assassins of Hassan ibn Sabah, "the old man of the mountain". Eventually, it all went far in consolidating the "black legend" of the Templars as an order of heretics. In fact, the French King, Philip the Fair, would later use these arguments, among others, to proscribe the Order.

As mentioned, Templars participated in numerous battles. To gain an idea of the extent of their commitment, 13 Knight Masters out of a total of 23 were killed in battle.

As an anecdote, one should mention the siege of Ascalon, a Fatimite city in the middle of the Frankish possessions.

After many days of siege, the Crusaders eventually created a breach in the wall with their war machines. William of Tyre, the Crusader chronicler, who did not think highly of the various Orders, wrote, "Bernard de Tremelay, the Temple's Great Master, advanced with his men and placed himself just at the breach so no one could enter they did. He did this to gain more plunder. 40 Templars entered through the wall, while the remainder guarded the breach thus preventing any other Crusader to follow them. The Turks were astonished to see this. All the Templars were slain, along with their Knight Master that day."

From this, it can be deduced that fear was not part of the Templar Brothers make up, nor did the approbation of other Crusaders bother them. It seems absurd to think that an experienced Knight Master like Tremelay, could think that he could subdue the city with a mere 40 knights. The situation can be viewed in a different and more logical way.

When the wall was breached, the Templars, as was usual, were in the van. They entered the fortification, with the plunder in mind, and were followed by the Crusaders. Tremelay prevented the Crusaders from entering the city as he felt that the disorganized Crusaders would not effectively be able to subdue the city. The Grand Master and his band then fought their way forward until they entered a small square and found themselves surrounded by Turks..... and were all killed.

There are many obscure and ambivalent stories like this in the Templar history, and each contributed to its eventual ruin.

Detail of a fresco from the templar Cressac chapel.

THE TEMPLARS' ENEMIES

During the time of the First Crusade, the Seljuk Empire (between present day Iraq and Iran) was breaking up and had lost control over Turkey and Syria.

In this area, power was shared among Turkish the tribes, Armenians, Kurdish and Arabs, all fighting each other in order to control the land, castles and cities.

On the other hand, Egypt was under the thrall of the Fatimite Caliphate, who were Shia Muslims, followers of Mohammad's son-in-law, Ali.

The Cairo-based Caliphs were attempting to consolidate their territories, rather than conquering the world as Saladin did later and putting pan-Islamic ideas to work.

The first army faced by the Crusaders was the Seljuks of Rum in Anatolia. There were Turcoman warriors in their ranks that made the Crusaders' campaign very difficult. They were mounted archers, equipped with deadly, small, curved bows that had a power never seen before.

The traditional Seljuk's military ranks, maintained by preceding dynasties, were organized as follows: professional horseman called Ghulams, some mercenary troops and a tribal group (generally Turcoman) as auxiliary troops.

The infantry was composed of indigenous warriors and Turcopoles.

It could be heavy infantry like those on the left, armed with a large shield, lances and pikes and protected by chain mail or metal plate. In their ranks, the infantry had also archers, crossbowmen, and Greek fire launchers.

The cavalry was not as heavy as the Christian ones, although they were heavily armed. Among them were included Ghulams, lancers and the feared mounted archers. In the illustration can be seen these charging horsemen who had also mastered the art of firing their bows on the move. Their method of fighting was to attack the Christian armies, using the technique of hit-and-run.

Muslim armies were organized into regiments with a structured chain of command. On the other hand, the Christian armies reflected contempory European medieval structures.

Christian troops were from diverse origins and obeyed only their liege Lords. This lack of cohesion made the discipline of the Templar squadrons even more valuable.

The Muslim army had to cover around 30 kms. per day, and then form a camp each evening. They made a circle of their tents, placing the Commander's tent in the center. If danger threatened, a trench was dug around the camp, or a series of pikes was placed around the camp.

Egypt and Syria became reunited under Atabeg Nur el Dim, a Syrian political warrior able to defend Islam.

His governor in Egypt was the young Salah al Din Yusif ibn Ayyub, known as Saladin to the Christians. Here he is seen in the accompanying illustration as an army commander under the umbrella.

In a remarkably short period of time, Saladin became the most powerful, as well as a highly popular leader.

Nur el Din envied the talents and success of this talented Kurdish man. He wanted rid of him but, for him anyway, death intervened before he could accomplish his wishes.

Following the Sultan's death, Saladin became the supreme Islamic governor of the area, founding the Ayyubida dynasty. Having surrounded the Frankish states, as the Muslim called the Crusaders, with his own dominion, in 1187, he eventually defeated and expelled the Christian army after the Battle of Hattin.

Saladin was, without doubt, the most prominent figure during the Crusades, or Frankish invasion. He was an exceptional politician and military leader, a man of high moral values and qualities of judgment that made him an admired figure throughout, not only the Muslim world, but also the Christian one.

TEMPLAR MILITARY TACTICS

To be a Templar knight required among other things a clear promise of military vows. These were to fight for the Holy Sites, to renounce any ransom if captured, never to rule a battle, they could not demand a ransom for a captured infidel, and vowed to defend any Christian if they were attacked by Muslims.

The cavalry regiment was at the centre of power and it comprised in the region of 300 heavy cavalry, armed with lancers and supported by additional personnel and the necessary logistics for a force of such size.

The Knight Marshal, as said earlier, was the military chief. Among his duties were the collection and distribution of all the military equipment. He also assigned the saddles and undertook the care of all the animals sent to the Middle East by the European states.

Templars were not allowed to choose their horses. If they did, they would be given the worst one. If, on the other hand, they had any problems with a horse, it being recalcitrant or lazy for example, they could request a replacement.

Horses were classified into three categories: For jousts, large and strong; medium and light horses, or steeds were good for war and, last were the hack horse, a small ones and very useful for farm duties. These were also called villains.

Castilian King Alfonse X "The Wise". Miniature poems book where we can see Muslim and Christian troupes.

Being so dependant on the cavalry, campaigning was limited to the winter or the beginning of spring, because good pastures did not exist in the Middle East for feeding their horses. That said, further north of Syria in Edessa and Antioch, pastures were more abundant. Compared to Jerusalem, this was an advantage.

The Templar Order was innovative in the art of war. Thanks to its organization, they became one of the first regular armies of the time, specialized in logistics, uniforms and armament.

Templars added some Muslim characteristics to traditional medieval battle tactics. They developed the

XV century miniature representing Damietta's capture in Egypt, during the 5th crusade.

combined use of infantry and cavalry. In the beginning, knight squadrons rode, with the infantry in front, onto the open field of the enemy's territory. They rode with armour-plated infantry protecting them on all four flanks.

When charging, the infantry opened its lines to allow the knights to pass through. Of course, this tactic required excellent coordination in the command structure because, as usually happened, the infantry ruined the manoeuvre by getting in the way of the charging knights.

As time passed, the Muslims influenced the tactics and the Crusaders ended up placing the cavalry behind the infantry.

If we read a description of a cavalry charge in a manual at the beginning of the XX century, it would be valid for medieval times.

"When charging against cavalry or infantry, each man will ride towards the opponent with the strong determination of killing him… During the clash, if both armies are equally inspired, success will depend on the horses and the soldiers' competence with arms."

Another contribution of the Templars was the use of Turcopoles, an indigenous Syrian mercenary light cavalry. It has to be remembered that the Christian knight was a heavy horseman, unstoppable during the charge, but incapable of fast manoeuvring and clumsy. The Turcopole, on the other hand, armed with lighter equipment and combined with the strong Templar cavalry turned into a fearsome weapon.

The perfect synchronization between both the infantry and the light cavalry was a guarantee for success.

Templar militia had a hierarchy and excellent discipline, and was above average of contemporary armies. They were noble knights, proud, and used to receiving orders and obeying them without hesitation.

Another advantage was the use of standard military equipment, making the combat units more consistent. Continuous training made compact units of knights who used their swords everyday.

This sense comradeship and mutual cooperation throughout their life, differentiated them from other knights and army personnel. Most of the armies were made up of obligatory drafts or mercenary troops that did not become a cohesive part of the unit with the sense of purpose that characterized the military monks.

Charge by heavy calvary was the action more frequently use on the battlefield.

TRAINING FOR A TEMPLAR MILITIA

As mentioned earlier, the military force of the Order was the cavalry. Marching was done by walk or trot; the knights had the squires with lances in front of them, the shield and horses as a guide. In battle, the squires retired behind. The marching was undertaken in silence, with absolutely no noise at all.

The formation was structured as follow: A ten knight group called "Banners"; ten banners made a squadron and the contingent of five to ten squadrons was called a "Battle".

A brother could leave the formation to take care of his horse, his saddle or his armour or to assist a Christian if he was about to be killed. If he left the column for any other reason, he was penalized and had to continue the march on foot.

When the Knight Marshal gave the order to charge, all the squires organized into squadrons, as they had to charge behind the knights. If the Lord's horse was wounded or killed, the squire relinquished his horse to him. The remainder of the horses, including mules, were guided by a squire who followed the banner at a safe distance, in order and trotting.

Sergeants had to fight like the knights. Those without adequate protection, for example a helmet or chain mail, had to fight too also, were allowed to retreat if wounded.

At the start of the charge, the Knight Marshal took the "Beausseant", or lead banner, and passed it to a Knight Commander, assigning him ten knights for its protection. The Knight Commander usually carried another banner with him in case the Knight Marshal was wounded. If that occurred, he substituted the banner so that the knights always had a banner as a point of reference during the battle.

Choosing the exact moment to charge was very important, so that all the horseman reached the point of impact at the same time.

The rules stated that the Knight Marshal, or the most experienced Brother, decided the moment. Once the moment occurred, all ten knights must protect the "Beausseant", they had to remain close never leave it unprotected.

The remainder of the knights, riding on the four sides, tried to inflict the most harm on the enemy, while also assisting in the protection of the "Beausseant".

Once the charge was completed, the sergeants took up an important role with their ordered lines. They contained the enemy if he was victorious, or allowed the knights time to regroup so they could pursue the enemy.

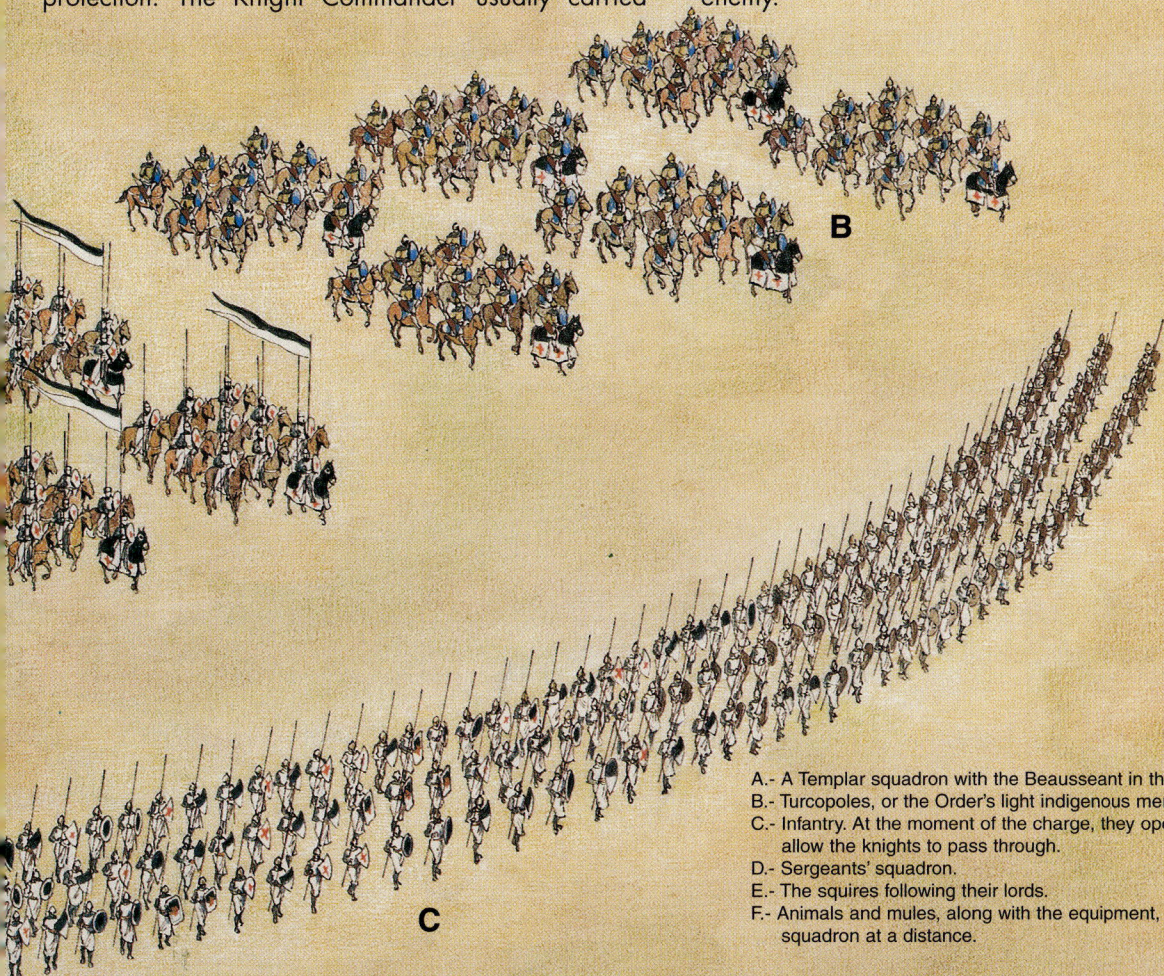

B

C

A.- A Templar squadron with the Beausseant in the centre.
B.- Turcopoles, or the Order's light indigenous mercenary cavalry.
C.- Infantry. At the moment of the charge, they open their line to allow the knights to pass through.
D.- Sergeants' squadron.
E.- The squires following their lords.
F.- Animals and mules, along with the equipment, following the squadron at a distance.

Solé-Amo

Templars were under the Grand Master's orders. He held absolute authority in the council, although under the Chapter's control when taking important matters.

At the Grand Master's death, and after the funeral, the election process began.

The Knight Marshal called all knights and sergeants to congregate in the Chapter. These knights in the assembly elected the Knight Commander who was to take charge of the Temple's seal; they will then congregate, in company with the Jerusalem, Antioch and Tripoli Knight Commanders, and select the election day.

They will fast on three consecutives Fridays …"To get God's advise and do the best for the house."

On Election Day, the chapter chose an Election Commander and his aide. The two candidates, "God and Justice Followers", to the repair to the chapel to pray and meditate until dawn.

Once the mass was over, they called the Election Commander and their companions and requested them to choose from among them their representatives.

They will choose neither "by pure love, favour nor by hatred."

First, there were two knights elected, then two more, until a total of twelve knights, in memory of the 12 apostles. These then elected the chaplain who represented Christ; there were 13 in total, 8 knights and 4 sergeants.

Finally, these 13 knights, in camera, chose the new Grand Master.

The Knight Commander then proclaimed the name of the chosen one and asked for approval. He then showed the newly-elected Grand Master to the assembled Order and said: ·Beautiful Brothers, thank God, here is our new Grand Master"

The Knight Master Gerard de Ridfort (1184-1189)

When King Baldwin the IV (the Leper) died in 1845, Count Raymund of Tripoli became regent. He was an honest and brave man and was trying to obtain a truce with Saladin to avoid loosing the kingdom. However, the opposing faction, lead by the Grand Master Ridfort who hated Count Raymond of Tripoli, favoured the accession of the incompetent Guy de Lussignan, the King's brother-in-law. By favoring this coronation, Ridfort followed his own personal dislikes instead of doing something good for Christianity.

Gerald de Ridfort was a vehement and proud man, and insensitive. He once sent ninety Templar horsemen, ten Hospitallers with their Master, Roger de Moulinsy, and forty horsemen to confront an army of 7,000 Saracens.

The Templar Marshal warned him against his foolish intentions whereupon the Grand Master retorted, "Do you really love that blond head of yours, that you want to keep it?"

The Knight Marshal replied, I will let them kill me like a knight and you will be the one running away from them'.

Those were prophetic words, the Grand Master and just two knights were the only survivors of the insane change.

Survivor is an adjective that can, with confidence, be applied to Gerald de Ridfort.

He pushed the King Guy into the Battle of Hattin, ignoring the truce agreed by Raymond and Saladin. The defeat at Hattin was overwhelming. Saladin let the thirsty Crusaders burn under the desert's sun, after crossing a desert territory.

The Muslim troops had no difficulty annihilating the demoralized and thirsty troops. The Muslim leader ordered the death of all captured men but left the Grand Master alive. He then set him free when Jerusalem fell.

During the siege of Saint John of Acre, this arrogant Grand Master once again fell into Saladin hands. This time the Saracen leader ordered his execution. However, to obtain his freedom, and his life, he agreed never to fight Islam again. This oath was in direct violation of the Templar vows.

TEMPLAR ECONOMY

It would not have been possible to maintain a military structure like the Templar Order without a solid economic structure.

Templars were aware of this since the foundation of the Order. This was the reason that the first Grand Master, Hugh of Payns, traveled to Europe with two clear objectives; to be recognized by the Church and to establish the firm economic foundations.

The Pope's support, along with a propaganda campaign during the beginning of the First Crusade, helped him to obtain very generous donations from the European ruling classes.

The magnitude of the donations surprised everyone. So much so that, and in a few years, they had to employ an administrator to manage all their possessions. France was very generous in donating money. However, other monarchies were equally generous thus establishing a strong bond with the Order.

King Saint Luis disembarkation in Damietta Egypt , 1249.

Istanbul, ancient Constantinople, ransacked during the fourth crusade.

Every Spanish kingdom fought constant battles with the Muslims. So, in order to gain support from these fearsome Warrior monks, the monarchs of Aragon, Portugal and Castile donated land and castles to the Order.

The Templar administration was a good example of their single-minded purpose.

They permuted, or sold fields and houses so as to group them in a single territory, thus facilitating its management and administration. They applied canons, or taxes to their possessions, with the sole purpose of not depending on the bad harvests or other factors that could harm their rents. The Orders' managers had a well-defined objective.

They had to assure self-sufficiency within their productive land in order to send the rent or leftover production to the army stationed in the Holy Land. The rents forwarded to the armies was sufficient for all its needs, thanks to the huge amount of arable land and cattle the Order possessed.

To keep the shipment of goods flowing, it was necessary to open commercial routes. These, thus, created the first Templar commercial routes equipped with control towers and shelters that protected the merchants from bandits and weather conditions.

There were mounted patrols along the routes, accommodation in fortresses acquired by the Brothers in strategically located areas for controlling the routes.

Two main roadways linked the north of France and the Mediterranean; One passing through the Paris headquarters and the other one from Payns.

All this wealth, protected by a solid military structure, won the merchant's confidence in both the Order and the Templar treasurers who acted as bankers.

In medieval Europe, all the international banking was carried out by the Italians. However, it was not long before the Templar infrastructure, along with honesty inspired by the monks, made them the bankers of Christendom.

The treasurers in the Paris headquarters were, from the XIII century administrators of the French King's treasury.

They gave loans, they extended letters of credit, they carried out collections and they carried out all types of banking services, turning their chapels into banking agencies.

It was also a priority to control maritime shipments in the Mediterranean, an essential and strategic support route for their armies in the Middle East. The Order was so efficient, that soon they had a fleet that rivaled the Venetian one. This helped them to compete for the commercial monopoly in the Mediterranean.

The Order became a multinational conglomerate of great importance during the time of the Crusades.

Templars got the control of the maritime traffic on the Mediterranean Sea rivaling with Venetians for the commercial routs.

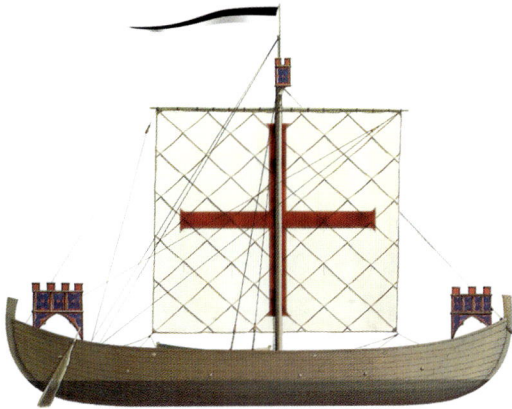

THE HOSPITALLERS

The order of Saint John's Hospital in Jerusalem was founded around 1070, when a group of Italian merchants founded the hospital in Jerusalem.

The hospital became affected by western immigration, and came under Catholic domination, administered by Gerard, in 1113. He, in turn, gained the Pope's recognition.

When the Templars became popular, the Hospitallers decided to convert the Order to a military one in order to receive similar donations, although they never abandoned charity and assistance.

Unlike the Templars, the Hospitalers admitted women, although exclusively for charitable services and the infirmary.

In 1306, the Order invaded the island of Rhodes where they established their headquarters. They later moved to Malta where they retained their independence and took up the title of Knights of Malta.

THE TEUTONIC KNIGHTS

Tradition associates this Order with the foundation of a German hospital in Jerusalem.

In 1191, they received the Pope's recognition as a religious order under the name Hospital of Saint Mary of the Germans of Jerusalem.

In the beginning, they gave medical and charitable assistance but, in 1198, they converted to a military order, giving birth to the Order of Teutonic Knights.

In accordance with the name, the members were mainly German knights and, as with the Hospitallers, they admitted women to be among their hospital personnel.

The Order grew strongly, mainly at the beginning of the XII century under the able direction of the Grand Master, Herrman von Salza.

After the fall of Acre, the Teutonic knights established themselves in Venice, and then later moved to Prussia, close to the Baltic Sea.

The Lutheran reform seriously affected the Order although it tried to re-structure to adapt to the times. However, it was all to no avail and it died out.

THE CALATRAVA ORDER

In Spanish Iberia, during the 1147, The king awarded the Templars the fortress of Calatrava on the Andalusian border.

For some obscure reason, typical of the Order, they soon abandoned the fortress, arguing that it was indefensible.

King Sancho of Castile, meanwhile, offered the Castle to "who feels ready to defend it". A monk from Navarre, Ramon Sierra, attended the Royal call and moved to Calatrava with his brothers and a contingent of soldiers.

In 1164, after the death of Ramon, the monks returned to Navarre leaving the castle to the soldier knights.

That same year, the new Grand Master, Don Garcia, adopted the Cistercian rules and through doing so, the Order was recognized by the Pope.

They later lost Calatrava to the Moors, but later, in 1212, they got it back. During that year, the Order became powerful in Castile.

From 1245, the King influenced the election of the Grand Master and, in 1476, he took the direct control of the order.

KNIGHTS OF SANTIAGO

They followed the Templars example; in 1158, a group of 13 Castilian Knights vowed to protect all pilgrims going to Santiago de Compostela.

A few years later, in 1171, these knights decided to take monastic vows under the rules of Saint Augustine. Recognition from the Pope followed later. Their duties were exclusively military, having their quarters in Montalban (Aragon). The Santiago Knights only admitted noblemen to their ranks. From the middle of the XIII century, the Crown appointed the Grand Masters and subsequently, from 1485, the king himself became the Grand Master.

MILITARY ORDERS

The Orders can be defined as religious institutions, approved by the Pope, and following the rules established by each founder or the adopted reforms.

Since the High Middle Ages, there were religious orders that inspired new ones, Saint Benito de Nursia, for example, founded the Benedictine order.

Due to the profound religious feeling of the time, many knights grouped into brotherhoods, where they shared a common life with the noble purpose of fighting for justice and to assist the helpless.

The Templar Order and the Santiago in Spain were created to protect the pilgrims.

To achieve this, the church had to do a great job in convincing the people.

Throughout the X and XI centuries, there were severe condemnations by the church against highway robbery. Named as "Capable of violating Christ's Peace", these sins were considered worst than being an infidel.

The romantic knights came into being with the idea of controlling the medieval cavalry under Christian ethics. By so doing, the Church acquired a moral authority over nobles and rulers. It tried to establish an autonomous Rome-based Papacy that did not hesitate to use military force to achieve its aims. From the beginning, the Catholic Church legalized the military orders and gave them privileges. In the case of the Templars, it came under direct Papal authority.

The Templars had to render accounts only to the Pope in Rome, which, per se, turned the Order into the military service of the Church.

At the close of the 11th century, the monastic orders were revitalized due to the spiritual reforms that shook the church.

In many respects, a monk can be considered a spiritual warrior who has abandoned worldly pleasures for a superior life.

By undertaking a Holy War and, aided by Crusader propaganda, they were able to make a bridge between the Christian monk, led by the Apostle of Love, and the deadly warrior.

Preaching by some visionaries, led by religious interest or power (a less evident one), managed to create a social acceptance for the Christian battle, even to the point of dying for it.

Among the Christian preachers during these Holy Wars should be mentioned Saint Bernard of Clairvaux, who was mentioned earlier.

"A new militia gender is born that was unknown in the past, destined to fight, without truce, against the malicious spirits that rule the air."

It is true, when I see fighting with a single corporeal force another corporeal enemy I do not see it strange or marvellous. When I see how this warrior soul fights the demons, it does not surprise me at all, though praiseworthy, the world is full of monks that hold that fight.

But, when I see men holding their sword with ardour and courage,

who would not judge them as unusual and praiseworthy?

An intrepid and brave soldier, that while covering his body with a steel amour; he keeps his soul under the faith's chain mail.

He can be sure that under these defensive weapons, he will not fear men or demons.

Even more, he does not fear death, he even want it!

What would scare him, death or alive, when he lives for Christ?

ESOTERICISM

Although templars were Christ's knights, lies turned them into the devil's worshipers.

The esoteric nature of the Order has given innumerable authors much to write about over the year.

There is already an extensive library, with new books published every year, on this subject alone.

While we wished to be objective when writing this book, we have come to recognize that there are a lot of aspects about these monks that are, more or less, disconcerting. Its origins and foundation are a mystery itself.

Hugh of Payns kept a mere nine knights for nine years, which hardly appears to be an adequate number of individuals to maintain the roads clear of danger in the Holy Land, its main mission. Why nine knights for nine years?

One of the common myths associated to templars was that they were the Holy Grail's beepers.

Did they really find a treasure in the Temple of Solomon?

Did they keep the Holy Grail?

Was there an obscure motive for the Order's meteoric rise apart of the economic reason mentioned earlier?

These and many more questions can be posed.

We cannot deny that obscurantism is one of the thorny aspects of the Templar's esoteric ways; some of the stories have their origins in the depraved minds of the medieval inquisitors who tortured the monks to obtain those infamous confessions.

One of the accusations derived from the inquiries, read torture, was one of idolatry.

It was said that Templars adored a decapitated head dubbed "Bafometo" that has been described in multiple ways.

At an esoteric level, the Bafometo represents reality. The collective and personal devil necessary to attain the light of knowledge.

The knight abandons the world of desire and conquers the flesh, in order to walk without ties along the silent knowledge; without God's guidance.

Laon's templar church.

For black magic, the Bafometo represents the origins of evil, the satanic goat of the sorcerers.

The initiation rites resemble those of a secret sect, a ritualistic and methodic rite full of symbolism and unknown to the world.

Another mystery around the Templars was the existence of a secret rule that could only be accessed by high dignitaries, which contradicted the Christian spirit.

The Order's rules prohibited the publishing of those rules and ordinances so no one outside the Order could read them.

In order to demonstrate that the Order had renounced the Christian dogmas, the Inquisitors associated the Templars with the Cathars. The Cathars held an interpretation of Christianity that had a stronghold in the French Occitain.

Thousands followed the sect from among both the rich and poor. The Cathari cult pushed the church to name it a heretic sect and to call a Crusade against it. In consequence they were almost exterminated. To accuse the Temple of Catharism implied being an heretic sect.

The Order's secrets pacts with the Muslims did not help them either; specially the one they signed with Hassan Ibn Sabbah, the "old man in the mountain", the chief of a sect of assassins; this sect also becomes lost in the esoteric mist.

And there's more, much more…

There was a coincidence in numbers, the fact that there were twenty-two Grand Masters. There are twenty-two letters in the Jewish alphabet and the Kabala tree of life.

There are twenty-two High Arcane in the Tarot, and twenty-two Apocalypse Books of Saint John.

The Order is also associated with the Priory of Sion, a secret order in Jerusalem founded by Godfrey of Bouillon and established at the Abbey of Our lady of Sion.

The Temple would be something like the military arm of this strange order of confused origins. It is believed that three of the founders of the Temple belonged to the Sion Order, among them Hugh of Payns.

The attitude of the Grand Master, Gerard de Ridfort, who contributed to the lost of Jerusalem; he also took the Priory of Sion to renounce the Temple making a rupture between the two orders.

"A pact with the devil". Esoteric and magic was common on the people's minds during the middle ages.

THE END OF THE TEMPLE

In 1291, after the fall of Saint John of Acre, the Templars moved to Cyprus. Having lost all Crusader states and the Holy sites and those being the ultimate purpose of the Order, a dilemma was posed to the Templars.

What would be the new purpose for the brothers?

There were three answers to that question.

To remain in Cyprus and attempt to re-conquer Jerusalem, an impossible task for anyone at the time, to go to Spain and join the Iberian Crusade, or retire to France, where they had enormous possessions. In the end, they opted for the third proposal, thereby signing their own death warrant.

As we have said before, the wealth of these warrior monks provoked envy among the European powers. It has to be taken into account, in the XIII century, the Templars were capable of raising an army of 15,000 men, well equipped and united by a single command with a common purpose.

In the Europe of the day, there was not a single power capable of doing the same.

While they were a neutral force during the political conflicts of the time, it must be assumed that behind their immense economic and military power, lay a hidden agenda.

The Templars nurtured an ideal that had nothing to with esoteric ideas. Their ideas could, in fact, be related to ideals of the present day. Nothing less the creation of a new world order, an international brotherhood united by the love of Christ, and ruled by the values of the austere military order.

The powers of medieval Europe, including the Church itself, and, believe it or not, public opinion, allowed the Order to grow. This was due mostly to what the Order achieved during the Crusades in the Holy Land. However, now that war was over, what could possibly justify such power?

To these two factors, the end of its fundamental purpose and its suspicious power, must be added a third factor.

It was that of the personality of the last Grand Master, a pious, simple but honest man who lacked the necessary strength to face the lies against the Order.

Would another Grand Master have been able to prevent the disaster that that was about to befall the Order?

Perhaps, perhaps not, but one thing is certain, Jacques de Molay certainly did not know how to prevent it.

Phillip IV "The Fair", was responsible for the end of the Order. He was suspicious, his coffers were empty, and he wanted the Templars' wealth.

He could not subordinate the Order to his Royal power, so he decided to put an end to it.

First, it was necessary to strip them of the Roman Pope's support. Phillip's ambition took him to plot inside the Roman Curia; by bribing the Curia he managed to move the Papacy to the French city of Avignon, thus placing the Pope under his control.

When he had all the strings together, William of Nogaret, the King's counsellor, began the insidious campaign of lies against them. In this, he sought the support of a renegade brother, Esquino de Floyran. The Pope, Clement V, although loyal to King Phillip, refused to take part in this infamous purpose.

The King then asked the Inquisition, which held political and religious jurisdiction throughout France, to sign an order to apprehend all the Brothers and to seize their wealth. It was the year 1307.

At this point, the long process began against the Brothers and their Grand Master. They were systematically interrogated and tortured.

Their tormentors extracted the most absurd confessions that, over time, created the mysterious Templar legends. The Grand Master himself, broken by fear and pain, eventually signed a document that called the Order heretic and blasphemous.

It is said, among others, that the Brothers were forced to spit on the crucifix to enter the Order. The Kiss of Brotherhood and Love given to the new member on acceptance into the Order, became transformed into a lustful act.

In April 1312, Pope Clement V, under pressure from the King, relinquished the Papal throne and published the bull, Vox Clementis, suppressing the Order.

Two years later, on an island in the Seine, Jacques de Molay and many of his Brothers died in a pyre for retracting their declarations and proclaiming their innocence, and also that of the Order.

The last Grand Master, 73 year-old Jacques de Molay, when he realized his position, recovered the knightly virtues and its sense of honour that was the cornerstone of the Order. In the end, he revealed the truth and paid with his life.